VOLUME TWO
Jam Trax
GUITAR METHOD

GUITAR METHOD

by Ralph Agresta

More advanced soloing ideas and more advanced chord playing ideas. Contains actual *JamTrax* jams, more tips on soloing, and more rhythm examples. Prepares you to join in on the fun of the *JamTrax* jam-along packages.

Cover instruments owned by Scot Arch
Photographed by William H. Draffen
The Washburn guitar appears courtesy of Washburn International

Project editor: Ed Lozano
Interior design and layout: Len Vogler

Order No. AM 940357
US International Standard Book Number: 0.8256.1586.0
UK International Standard Book Number: 0.7119.6113.1

Exclusive Distributors:
Music Sales Corporation
257 Park Avenue South, New York, NY 10010 USA
Music Sales Limited
8/9 Frith Street, London W1V 5TZ England
Music Sales Pty. Limited
120 Rothschild Street, Rosebery, Sydney, NSW 2018, Australia

Printed in the United States of America by
Vicks Lithograph and Printing Corporation

Amsco Publications
New York/London/Sydney

CD Track Listing

Contents

How to Use This Book

This book is divided into two sections: "Playing Chords" (rhythm playing) and "Your First Solo" (lead playing). Each of these sections is preceded by a few pages of basic information which you should read over before attempting to play the actual musical examples that are featured on the included CD.

Don't worry if initially you don't understand everything presented in the basic information sections. All you really need to get started is an understanding of *tablature* and *chord diagrams* (which are both easy to understand and are clearly explained in the beginning of this book) and a pair of ears (so you can listen to the recorded examples on the CD). Each example featured on the disk is recorded in a stereo split so that you can 'pan' to the left or right side to either isolate the guitar part for a better listen or to isolate the backing track (which is anything from a simple drum beat to a full band backup) in order to play along.

Throughout the "Playing Chords" section of the book you'll find a good selection of chords introduced in the form of exercises, 'song sound-alike' chord progressions, various songs, and actual *JamTrax* jams.

Each example that you play, starting with "Rhythmic Notation (Slash Note Values)," should be thought of as a separate lesson. Take your time to read over the text that precedes each musical sample. Whenever a new chord or scale is introduced, spend some time memorizing the correct placement of the fret-hand fingertips. Each fingering should be thought in terms of:

- Which fingers am I using?

- Which string(s) is being pressed down?

- At which fret is each finger placed?

Also, take note of which strings are not being played at all (indicated in the string diagram by an X located over the unused string). Each chord shape should be learned to the point where it can be recalled and played simply by recognizing the chord name.

The "Your First Solo" section is also preceded by a few pages of basic information that will increase your understanding of music and help to prepare you to grow as a musician. If, at any point, you find this at all tedious and want to jump right into trying to play a solo, you can skip ahead to "Introducing the 'Box' Pattern" where you can get used to playing single notes by practicing these very simple scales. Be aware that single-note fingerings are indicated by the small numbers located near the noteheads in the standard notation. Your next step will be to focus on the 'box' pattern featured in the list of "Scales and Techniques" that precede each solo. Try mixing up the order of notes within the 'box' and play them randomly until you can play any note in the scale at will. This kind of preparation will go a long way in enabling you to play your first solo.

As for technique, the TV can serve as a good teacher. Just take a look at MTV, VH1, the various country music stations, and any other shows that feature music, and you'll see more than enough guitarists. Watch them closely to see how the guitar is held and to learn the proper placement of the hands and fingers. Remember though that there are numerous variations of guitar technique, so check out lots of players. If you don't have a teacher to guide you, do what works and feels good to you.

Having said that, here are a few technique tips. When *fretting,* or pressing down on notes, keep the inside of the fret-hand rounded (as though you were holding a softball) as you focus accurate downward pressure on the strings with the fingertips. Many beginning players wrongly overcompensate for bad technique by simply squeezing the neck harder which often results in hand fatigue and unclear or sloppy sounding chords. Check to see if you're playing a chord cleanly by playing each note of the chord separately as you hold the chord shape. If you hear any buzzing or muted notes adjust your fingers accordingly.

The pick is held between the thumb and the side (or tip) of the index finger of the pick-hand. When holding the pick over the strings, think of the relationship between the pick and the strings as you would a needle and a record. Again, it is important to experiment to find what is comfortable for you.

Most of all, remember to take your time, be patient, and practice, practice, practice. The toughest part of playing any instrument is in the beginning when you're just getting started so . . .

Good luck, have fun, and, as always, I sincerely hope that you enjoy and learn from this book and CD.

More Chords and Techniques

The B7 Chord

Once you know the B7 chord, you can use it with the E7 and A7 chords that you learned in Book 1 to play a blues progression like this in the key of E. Thousands of songs and jams are based on these three chords. This particular chart is for the very first *JamTrax* jam ever recorded, which is track 1 on the CD that comes with the *Blues JamTrax for Guitar* package. Obviously you don't need the backing track to practice and learn this exercise but it makes it more fun.

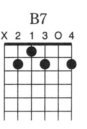

12-Bar Blues

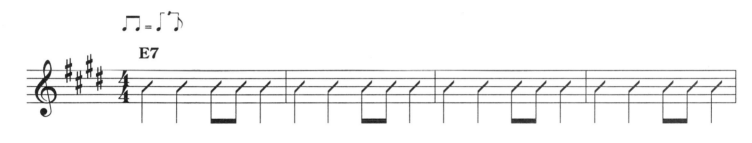

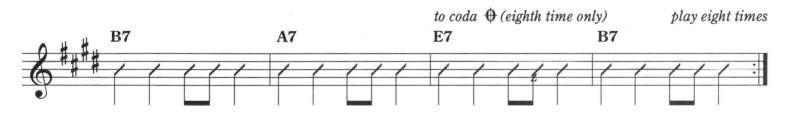

Another E7 and A7 Chord Shape

For a little change of flavor, feel free to substitute these voicings for the first ones you learned.

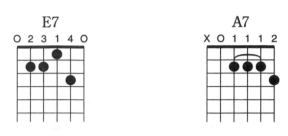

Other *JamTrax* Jams Based on the E7, A7, and B7 Chords

"12-Bar Boogie Shuffle in E"	*Blues*
"Another Joy"	*Modern Blues*
"Slow 12-Bar Blues in E"	*12-Bar Blues*
"Fast 12-Bar Blues in E"	*12-Bar Blues*
"12-Bar Southern Blues with Stops in E"	*12-Bar Blues*
"Back Against the Wall"	*Chicago Blues*
"Candy Apple Coupe"	*Chicago Blues*
"R.A.'s Boogie in E"	*More Blues*
"My Muddy Waters"	*More Blues*
"Rockabilly Truth"	*Country*

The Ballad of Ron and Coco

As we see in the next example, the E and A major chords may be substituted for the E7 and A7 chords without changing the basic progression. In "The Ballad of John and Yoko," John Lennon used a busier strum pattern with our three magic chords in the key of E much like we did here.

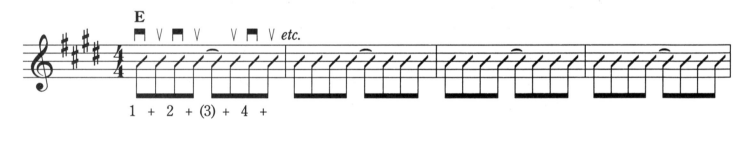

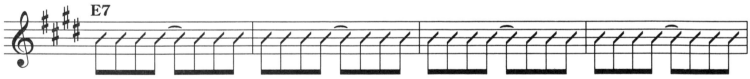

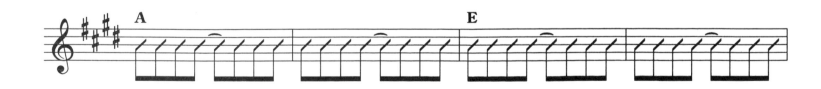

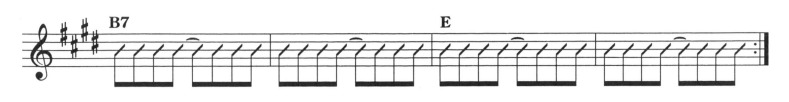

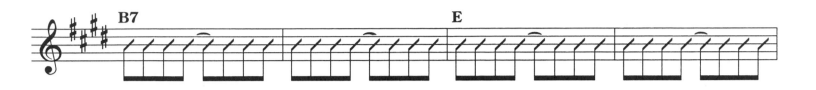

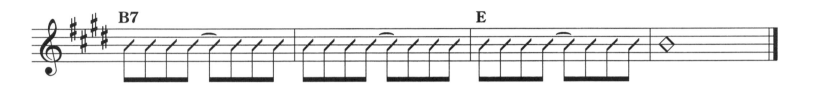

Please Excuse Me

The last E blues progression that we'll be looking at is "Please Excuse Me," which is the original *JamTrax* jam that we've included on the CD that comes with this book. It was originally featured on the *More Blues JamTrax for Guitar* disk and was modeled after Eric Clapton's "Before You Accuse Me."

As you play along with the included track, remember to have fun with the strum. Try to make it move with the flow of the drums and the bass. Every now and then as you repeat the choruses or cycles of this jam, try substituting the E and A major chords in place of E7 and A7 chords. Or you can apply the *low/high strum technique* (discussed in Book 1). Also, try accenting what you feel are the strong beats with a slightly harder than usual strum. Or if you like you can try to keep all of the strums perfectly equal in volume. Don't be afraid to experiment. When it comes to rhythm playing the old saying, "if it feels good; do it," definitely applies.

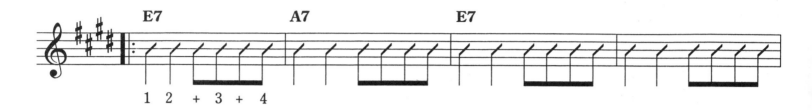

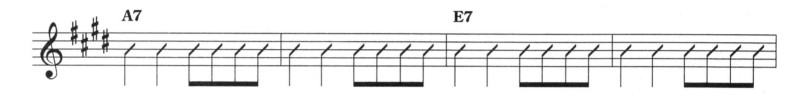

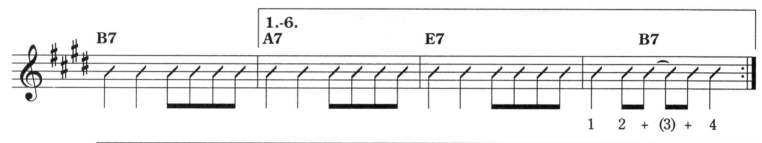

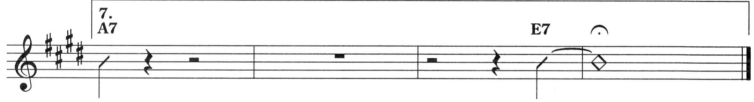

Please Excuse Me with Diads

You can also use the following kinds of *diads* (two-note chords) to play a second, completely different rhythm part for "Please Excuse Me." First, let's learn these simple E5, E6, A5, A6, and B5 chord forms. Keep in mind that the numbers that you see next to the standard notation noteheads indicate which fret-hand fingers you should use. Here's an important tip: Do not release pressure on whatever note your first finger is playing when you switch to your third finger to play either the E6 or A6 chord.

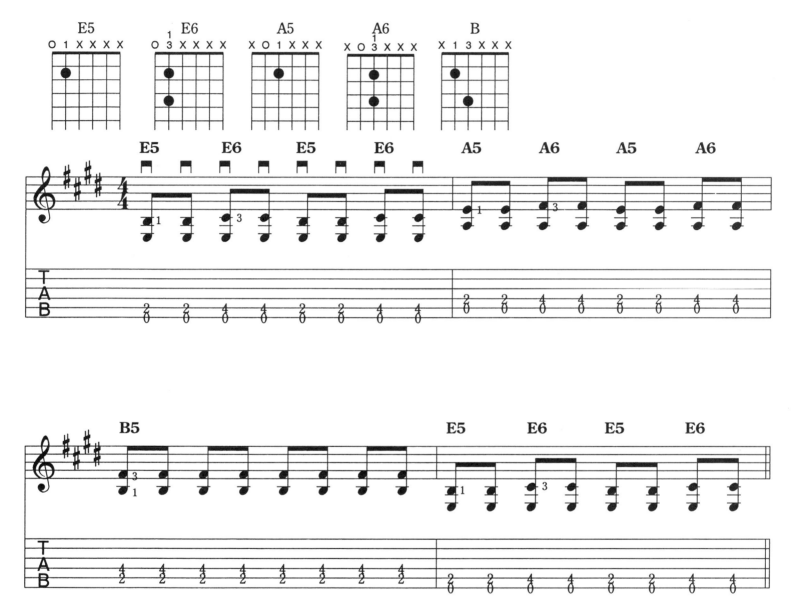

Please Excuse Me with an Alternate Rhythm

Now let's use diads to play the second rhythm part for "Please Excuse Me." When you're comfortable with both rhythm parts, feel free to alternate between them as you jam with the live track.

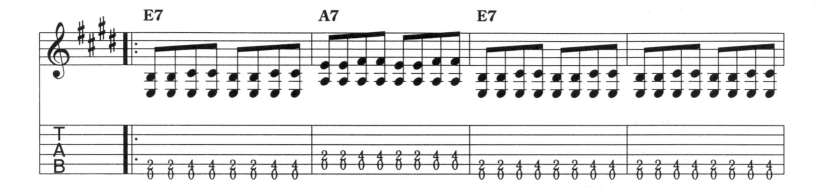

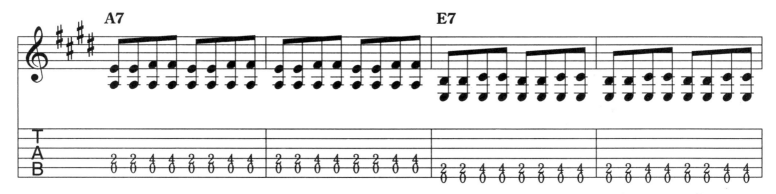

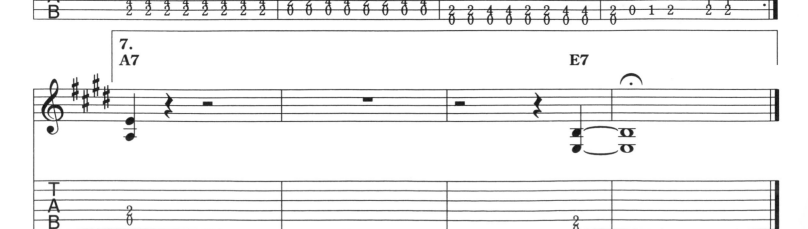

The G7 and C7 Chords

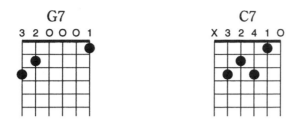

Love Me Don't

We'll be using these two new chords and a strum pattern that's two measures long to *establish a groove* (play a rhythmic style) like the one you hear on the Beatles' "Love Me Do." This exercise also conveys a decidedly country rhythm guitar style.

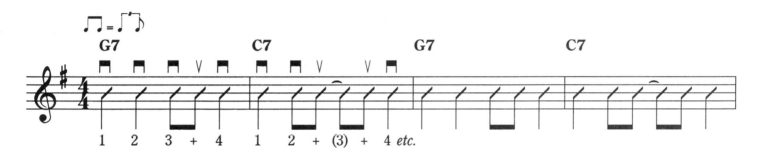

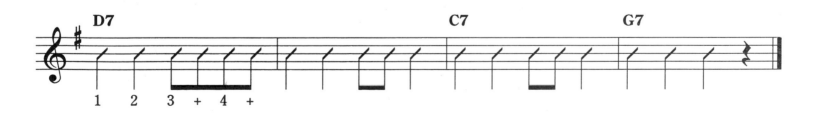

The Fmaj7 and G6 Chords

When we play this first-position F major seventh (Fmaj7) chord form in the third position it becomes a G sixth (G6) chord. The fret-hand thumb may be used to play the optional sixth-string-root note for each of these chords. If you find the root note too difficult to play, simply mute the string by touching it with the thumb just enough to stop it from ringing.

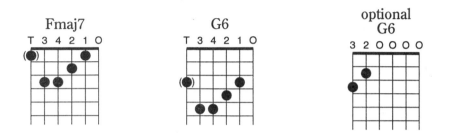

Nightmares

Now we'll use these two chords and another two-measure rhythm pattern to lay down a groove like the one that dominates the track of the Fleetwood Mac hit "Dreams."

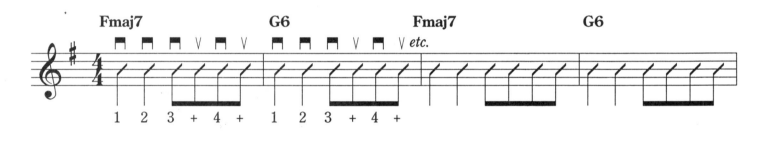

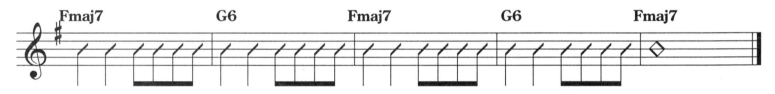

All along the Stairway

Do you remember the open Am and Em7/A chords from Book 1? We're going to use them with the Fmaj7 and G6 chords from "Nightmares" to play the kind of chords that you've heard in Bob Dylan's "All along the Watchtower" or Led Zeppelin's "Stairway to Heaven."

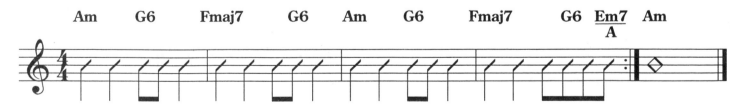

The $\frac{C}{G}$ Chord

The G note included in the bottom of this form makes this a very full-sounding version of the C chord. Study the similarity in the fingering of this $\frac{C}{G}$ chord and the Fmaj7 chord that we used in the last two examples. In Lou Reed's "Walk on the Wild Side," a busy rhythm like the one you see here is teamed up with the $\frac{C}{G}$ and Fmaj7 chords to create the song's rhythmic foundation.

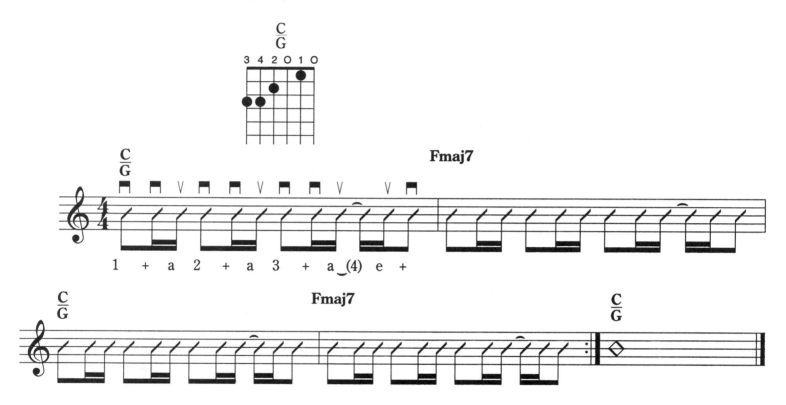

The D+ Chord

In Eddie Money's "Baby Hold On" the D and D augmented (D+) chords are alternated to form a verse groove that sounds similar to this rhythmic exercise.

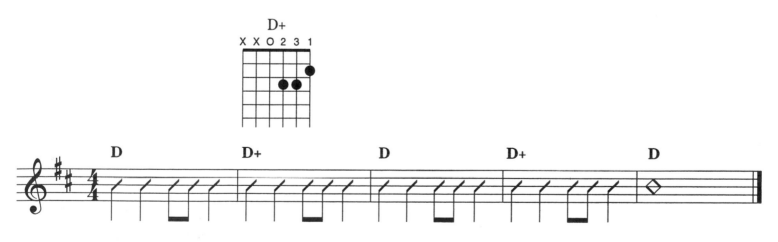

The D6 Chord

The D+ chord is a chord of movement that is often used to lead either to or away from a D or D6 chord.

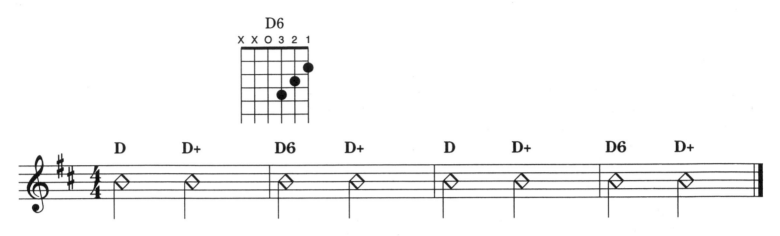

The A+ and A6 Chords

This form of the A6 chord requires you lay your first fret-hand finger flat across the first three strings at the second fret. You will probably have to drop the fret-hand thumb down behind the back of the guitar neck and keep a straight first finger to play all three notes in the *bar* cleanly.

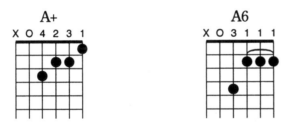

Starting Under

"Starting Under" is a combination of two standard chord progressions that utilize the A, A+, and A6 *chromatic* (featuring half steps) chord change. As you play these, imagine the intro to John Lennon's "Starting Over."

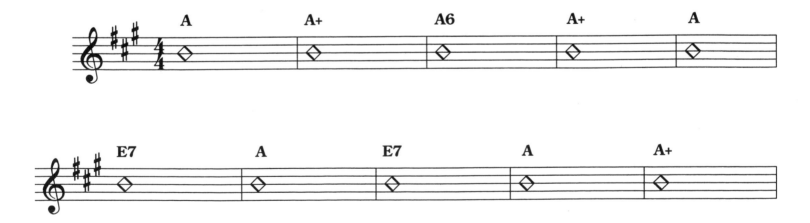

Because

For a while the Dave Clark Five were in direct competition with the Beatles (I guess we know who won). However, they did turn out lots of great songs including this one called "Because" which features a chord sequence built on A, A+, A6, and A7. (An extension of the previous chromatic chord changes.)

by Dave Clark

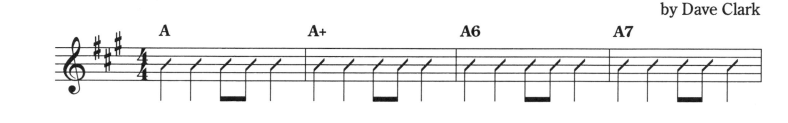

The Dsus4 and Dsus2 Chords

The Dsus4 and Dsus2 chords are often used to add color to the standard open D chord.

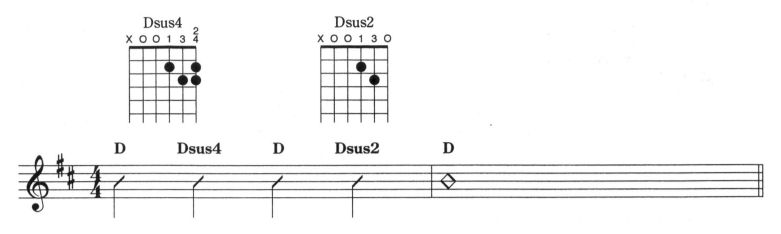

Playing the D, Dsus4, and Dsus2 Chords with Hammerons

When one chord is tied to another as we see in the following example, the second chord should not be strummed. In this situation we change from one chord to the next by sounding the second chord's altered note by "hammering" on to it with the tip of the appropriate finger.

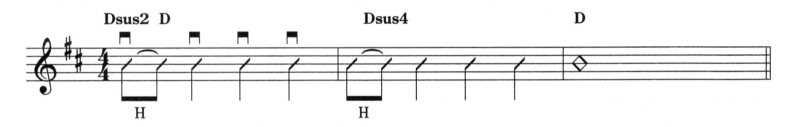

The 6/8 Rhythm

Music written in 3/8 or 6/8 time has a kind of waltz feel to it. The next four measures show the development of measure one's straight strum in 6/8 time. In 6/8 time we use six *rimshots* (or clicks) for the countoff.

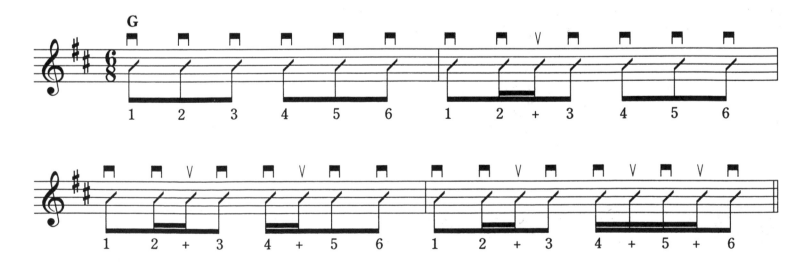

Lucky Man

Emerson, Lake and Palmer's "Lucky Man" is a great song to play on the acoustic guitar. It combines the § rhythms we just learned with the Dsus4 and Dsus2 hammeron embellishments.

by Greg Lake

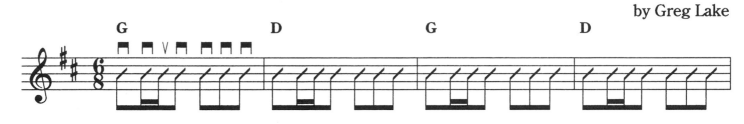

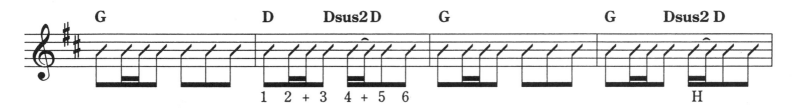

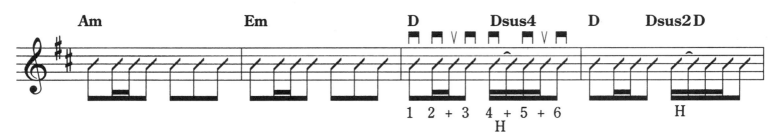

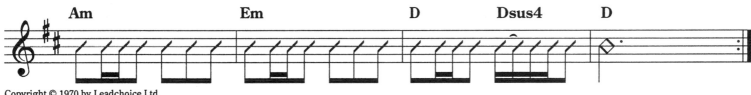

The F♯°7 Chord

The *diminished seventh chord* is also a chord of movement that tends to lead to the major chord whose root is one half-step higher. The next two bars we see the F♯°7 chord leading to the G major chord.

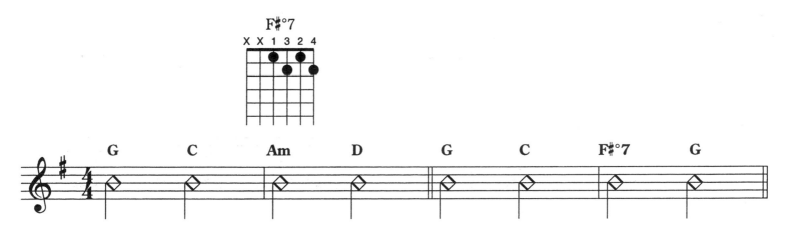

The G♯°7 Chord

This G♯°7 chord is the same form as the F♯°7 chord only this time it's played in the fourth position (two frets higher).

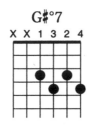

The Country Gentleman

Direct from our *Country JamTrax for Guitar* package, "The Country Gentleman" is a simple song that features the G♯°7 chord.

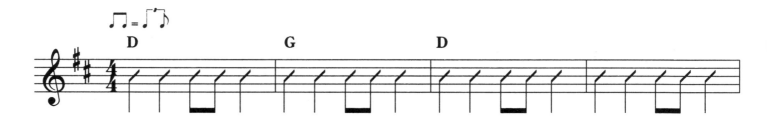

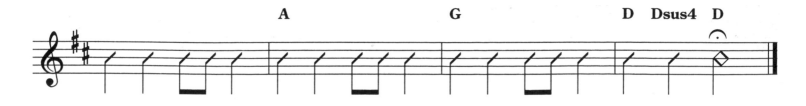

Alternating Bass Notes with Chords

Each of the main chords in "The Country Gentleman" is played here using
alternating bass notes and single strums. Once you know which bass notes to
play with each of these chords go back to "The Country Gentleman" chart and
play it using this rhythmic technique.

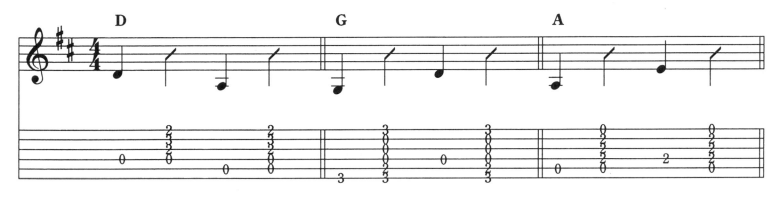

Anticipating the Downbeat

As we learned in Book 1, *anticipating the downbeat* is a fancy way of saying that
you should play the downbeat chord or note early. In the next few bars we are
playing each of the downbeat chords one eighth-note early so that all of our
chords are actually strummed on the previous upbeat.

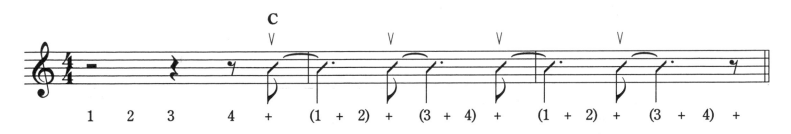

Combining the Anticipated Downbeat with the Muted Strum

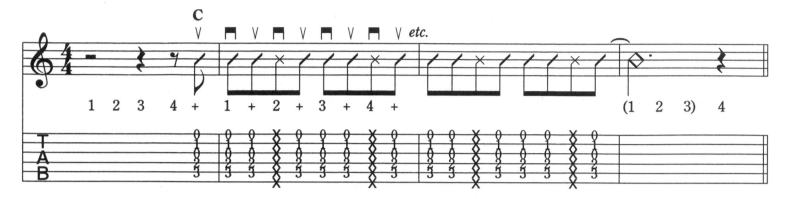

More than Chords

Here we can apply the use of the anticipated downbeat and the muted strum to chords that will allow us to emulate the kind of rhythm playing heard on Extreme's "More than Words."

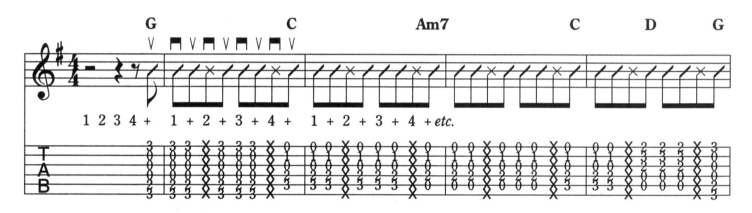

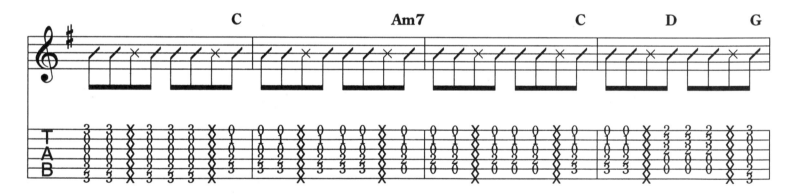

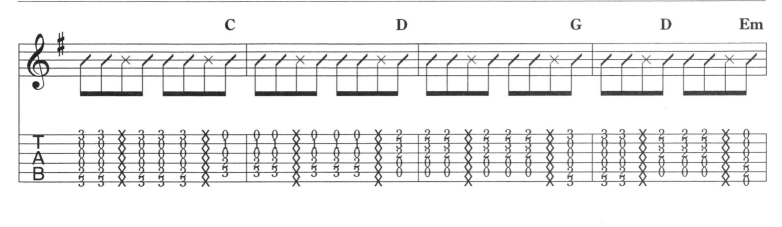

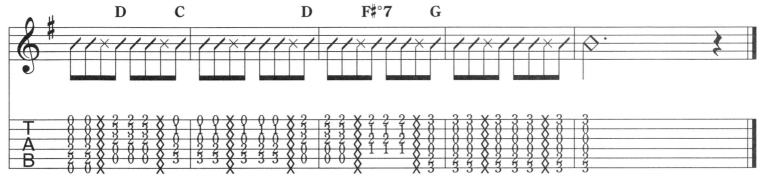

Bar Chords

The Sixth-String-Root Bar Chord Form

Your first full *bar chord* is a major form whose root is on the sixth string. As with all movable chord forms the name of the chord will change depending on where you place the root. Bar chords are usually a little harder to play than open chords, and you may have to make a few adjustments until you find the best way to hold your fret hand. Start by dropping the thumb to the center of the back of the neck and hold your hand the way you would to make a shadow puppet of a duck. Keep the first finger (the finger your going to bar with) as straight as possible but curl the remaining three fingers so you can play the unbarred notes with the tips of the second, third, and fourth fingers. When you slide this bar-chord shape up and down the fretboard (as you will in this next exercise), try to retain the chord shape in your hand as you release pressure on the strings. This will help you move quickly from one position to the next.

Notice that when we slide this bar-chord shape all the way down to the open position that we end up with a refingered open E chord. When playing this fingering of the open E chord, you might find it more comfortable to let your fret-hand thumb slide slightly up from the back of the neck. This exercise shows where to place our first bar shape to play the commonly used major chords whose roots are natural notes. Don't worry if you have trouble with any of these, they will take some time to master.

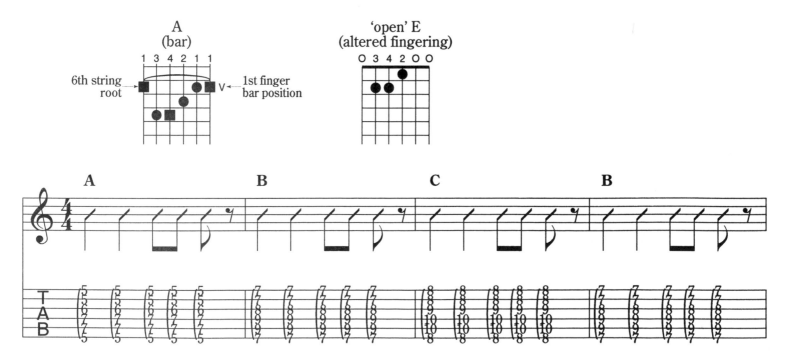

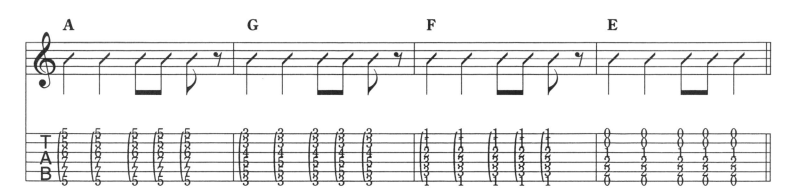

A Timeless Bar Chord Riff

Next we'll use this same bar chord shape to play the kind of chordal riff that was used by Green Day in "Brain Stew/Jaded" and Chicago in "25 or 6 to 4."

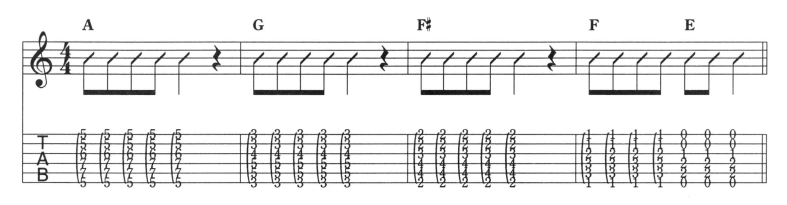

Other Sixth-String-Root Bar-Chord Shapes

Check out the similarity between these major, minor, minor seventh, and seventh chord shapes and the open E chord variations that you already know.

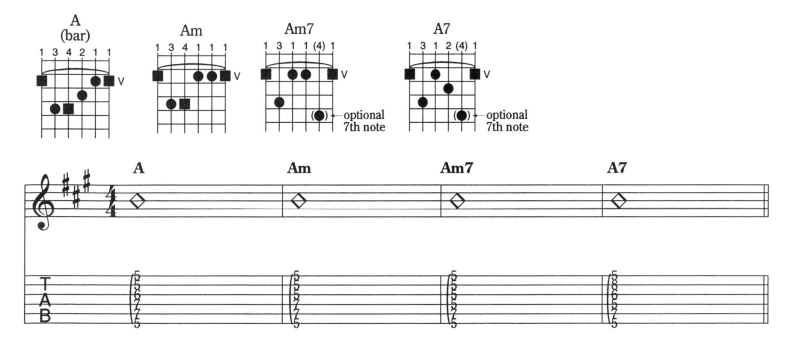

Minor Bar Blues

"Minor Bar Blues" is nothing more than a sixth-string-root minor bar-chord shape exercise.

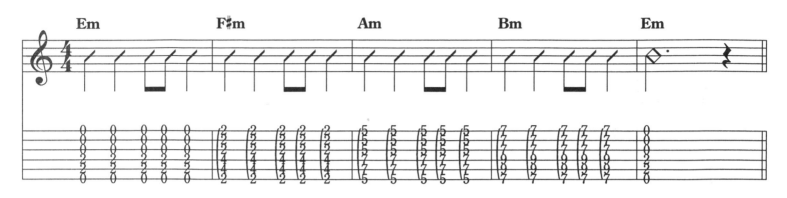

Santana–Style Blues

The sixth-string-root minor-seventh bar-chord shape and the arpeggio are both used here to play this latin/rock progression.

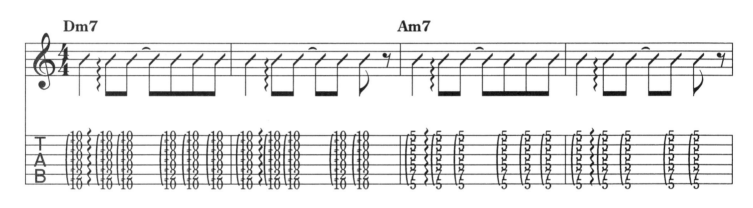

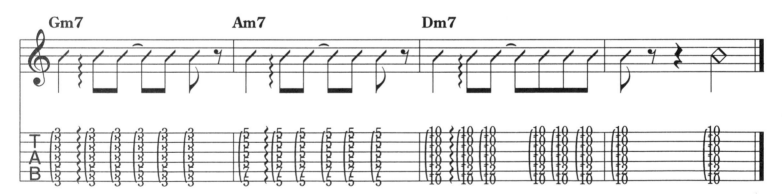

He's a Woman

The sixth-string-root seventh bar-chord shape (with the optional seventh note) is used to play this Beatle-style exercise.

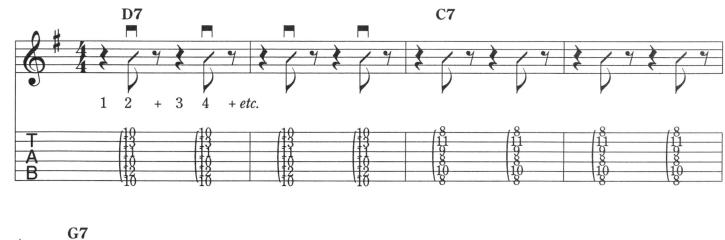

Here the sixth-string-root major and minor bar-forms are used to play the first six chords in the key of E.

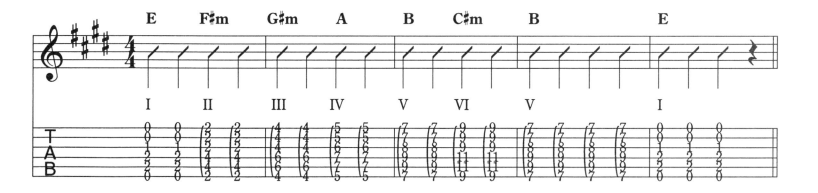

Beatlish Chords

The next chord progression features the open E chord and various major and minor bar chords arranged to simulate the kinds of chords (in the key of E) that were used by the Beatles and countless other groups. Again, in this situation it might help you to switch more easily to the sixth-string-root bar-chord forms if you use your second, third, and fourth fret-hand fingers to fret the open E chord. Try playing this first one with the tempo and the feel of the classic "Nowhere Man."

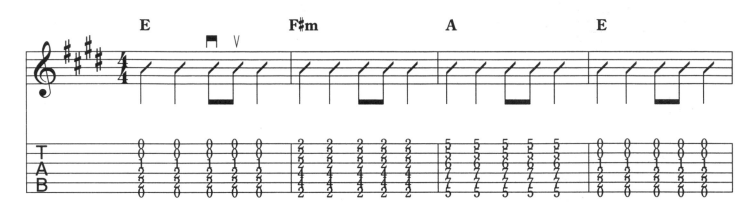

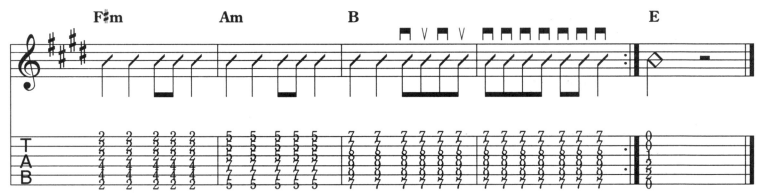

The Fifth-String-Root Bar-Chord Form

Our second bar-chord form is based on the shape of an open A chord.

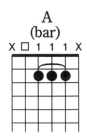

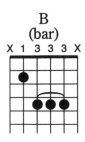

Here, the fifth-string-root bar-chord form is played in several positions to produce a variety of major bar chords.

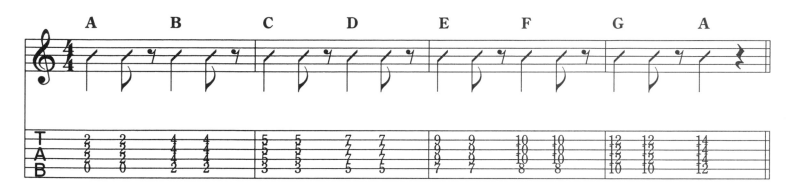

Rogaine

The fifth-string-root major bar-chord form is the only chord shape you'll need to play this rhythm guitar part which is a tip of the hat to Eric Clapton's crowd-pleasing version of "Cocaine." Remember to hold the shape of the chord with your fret hand as you release pressure when moving it from position to position.

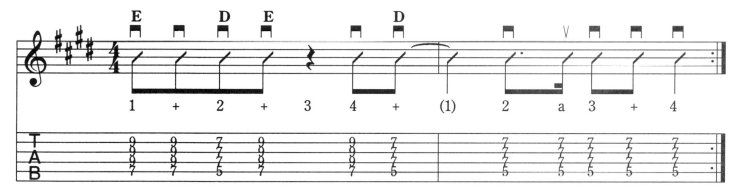

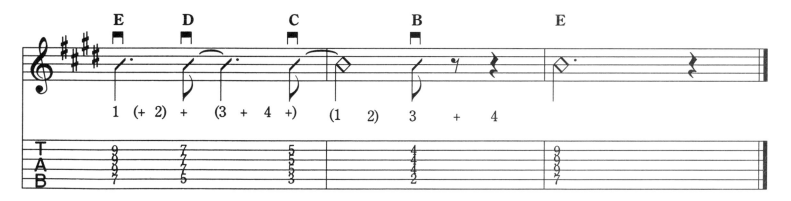

Three Other Fifth-String-Root Bar-Chord Forms

Here, our second major bar-chord shape is varied to produce the minor, minor seventh, and seventh fifth-string-root bar-chord shapes.

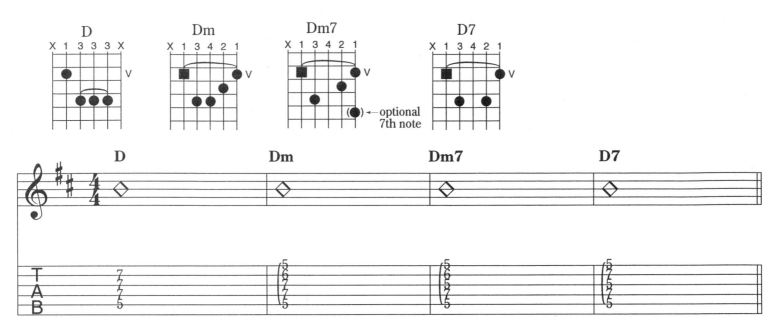

Combining the Major and Minor Fifth-String-Root Shapes

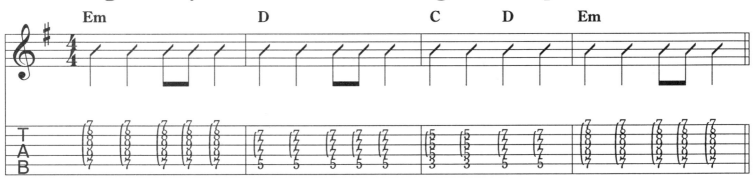

Rolling Stones–Style Rhythm

Both sixth- and fifth-string-root chord forms are combined for this Rolling Stones– style rhythm. If you're not sure which chord form or position to use, double check what you're about to play with what's written in the tablature.

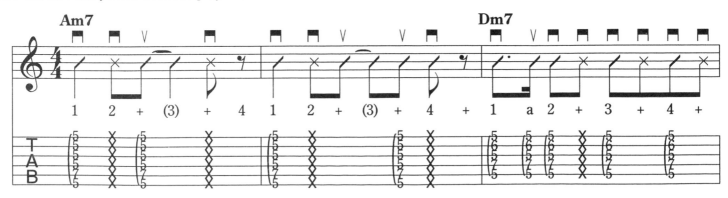

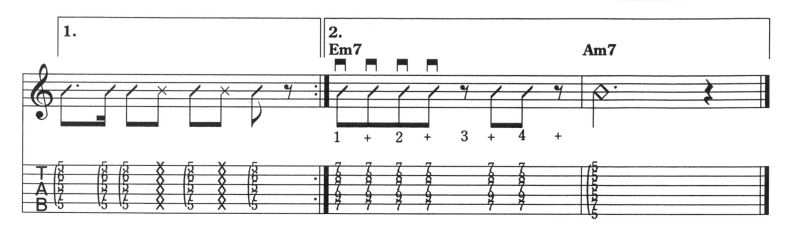

Pedal Tones

A *pedal tone* is a sustained or continuously repeated note that is often played in conjunction with one or more chords.

Neil Young–Style Rhythm

Here the sixth-string open E note is used as a pedal tone with the fifth-string root major bar form to play this fuller sounding version of one of the Neil Young–style rhythms that we played in book one.

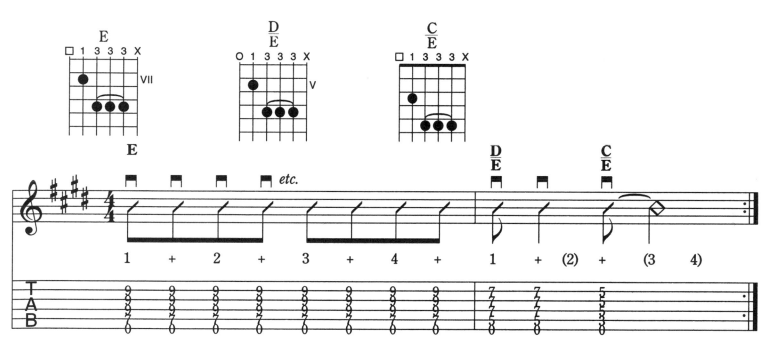

Led Zeppelin–Style Rhythm

Now we'll combine both major bar chord forms and the low E pedal tone to play a Jimmy Page–style riff. This is actually a good exercise to practice switching between the fifth-position D and A major chords.

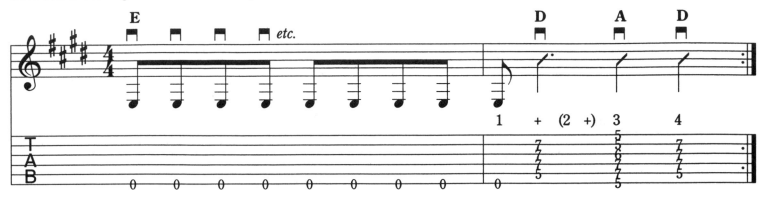

The $\frac{A}{A}$ Chord and the $\frac{G6}{A}$ Chord

These two chords are both played with the same simple chord shape. The fifth-string open A note, which serves as the root to both chords, is functioning as a pedal tone.

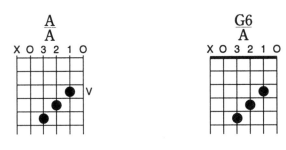

Let It Rain

"Let It Rain" is another one of Eric Clapton's best known songs. For this arrangement we've used chords with pedal tones, bar chords, and open chords. (*Note:* Open chords may be substituted for the bar chords given in measures 3 and 4.)

by Bonnie Sheridan and Eric Clapton

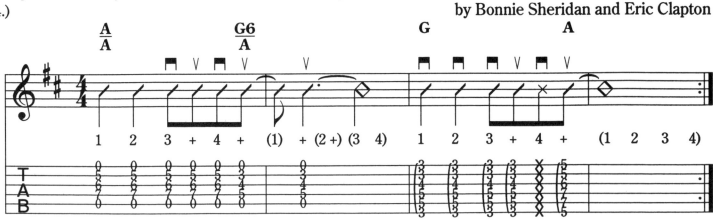

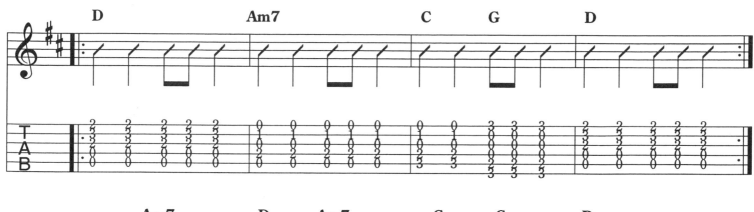

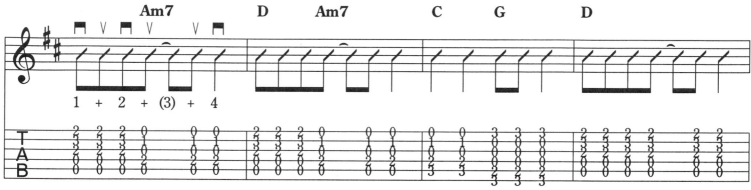

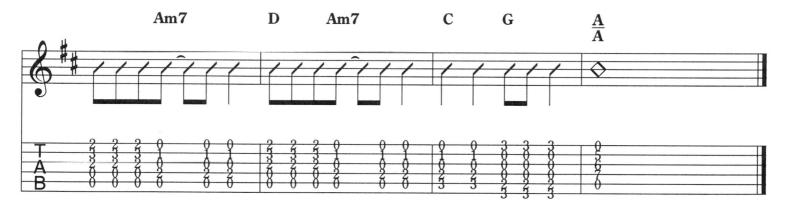

Broken Chords

A *broken chord* is a chord whose tones are sounded one at a time in succession.

House of the Rising Sun

This traditional folksong in § time was a big hit for Eric Burdon and the Animals and is well known by many guitarists who probably learned about broken chords by playing this particular progression.

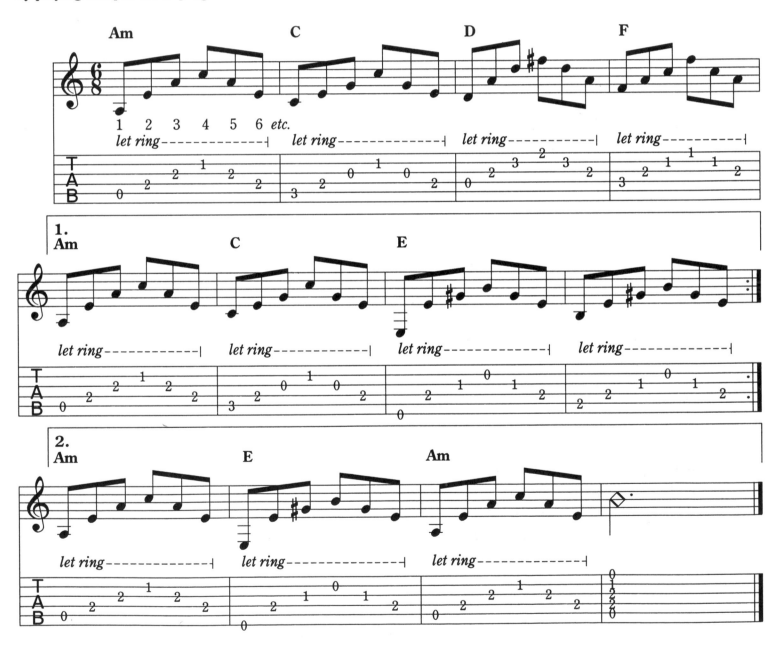

The $\frac{Am7}{G}$ Chord and the $\frac{D7}{F\sharp}$ Chord

Babe I'm Gonna Leave You

"Babe I'm Gonna Leave You" is another traditional folksong that features broken chords and chords with altered roots. Led Zeppelin popularized this song by recording a version of it on their first album. Notice how the thumb can be used in the optional fingering given for the F chord in measure 4. If you find this uncomfortable, you can use the old standard sixth-string-root major bar-chord form in the first position.

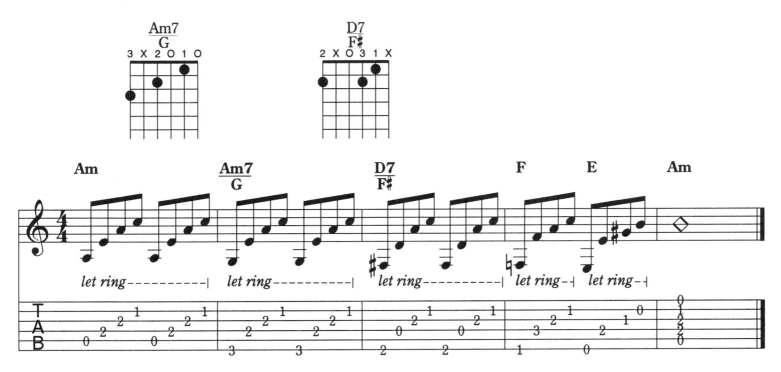

The Open Am7, Open $\frac{D\ add9\ add11}{A}$, and E7sus4♭9 Chord

When the open Am7 chord shape is moved up one whole step an interesting modal chord is formed. We're calling this chord a $\frac{D\ add9\ add11}{A}$ The highly exotic E7sus4♭9 chord has a shape that is similar to the diminished chords we saw earlier. Be careful to locate it properly.

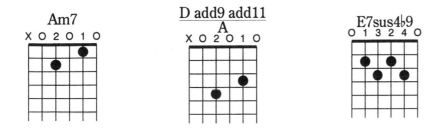

From the Beginning

by Greg Lake

This arrangement of Emerson, Lake and Palmer's "From the Beginning" brings together many of the rhythmic elements and techniques that we've studied so far.

The Guitar's Fourth Octave

The pattern of notes between frets 0 and 12 is the same as the pattern of notes between frets 12 and 24. The notes in the upper range will sound one octave higher.

The *8va* marking is often used to indicate that the notes so labeled should be played one octave higher.

See how the same pattern of notes (in this case the E chromatic scale), can be played one octave higher in the 12-through-24 fret range. (*Note:* Not all guitars have twenty four frets; just go as high as you can.)

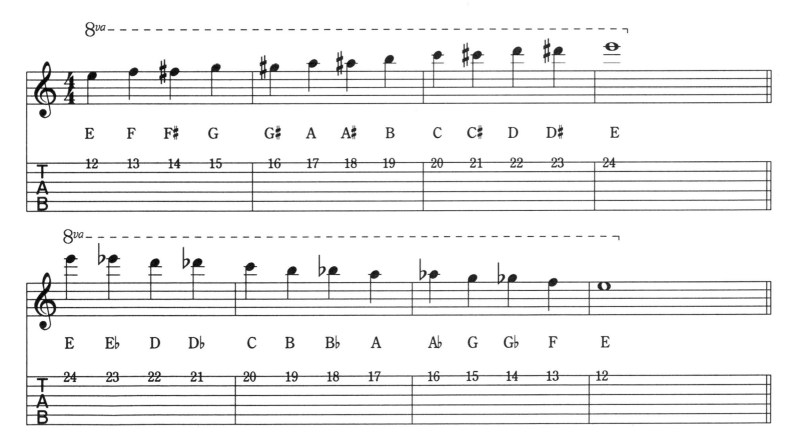

The Chromatic Fretboard Diagram

O.K. gang, here's the big picture! Obviously, the more you play, the more these notes will become familiar to you – so don't let yourself get too bogged down at this point. Study this diagram one string at a time and then move on. As with any other involved concept, you will need to review and digest this over time. Roman numerals are usually used to indicate frets or fretboard position.

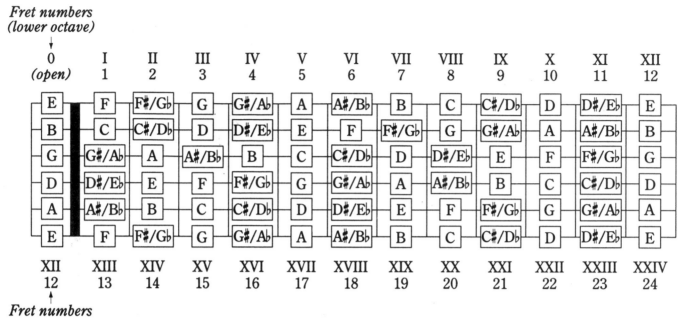

Fret numbers (lower octave)

Fret numbers (higher octave)

Basic Scale Theory

Scales are nothing more than a specific grouping of notes in a particular order. One way of thinking about scales is that they are all variations of the major scale. The distance between any two notes within a scale is called an *interval*. As seen below, the series of intervals or steps in a major scale is: whole-step, whole-step, half-step, whole-step, whole-step, whole-step, half-step. By varying the intervals of the major scale we can produce the many different scales that exist in music. The first note of any scale is called the *root* and is used to name the scale. A given scale can be played in any key by moving the root (and thereby the whole scale) to the pitch that has the same name as the key you want to play in. The following five scales represent what are probably the most often used scales in popular music. (*Note:* These scales are all single-octave scales laid out on a single string so that you can visualize the intervals.) Most of the scales throughout this book are laid out "across" the fretboard in single- and double-octave patterns that may seem larger or more complex. Don't be fooled, this is only because the given scale notes are played more than once in different octaves (or higher and lower tonal ranges).

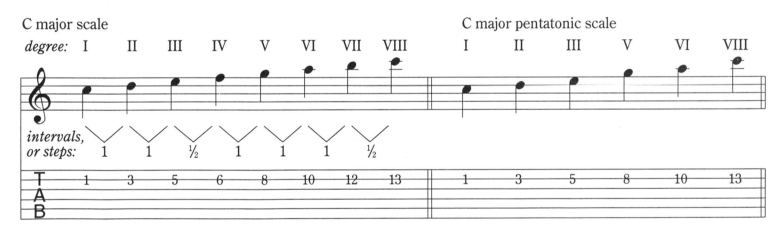

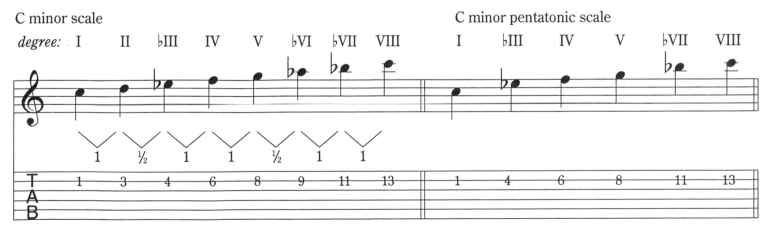

C blues scale
(minor pentatonic with flatted fifth note)

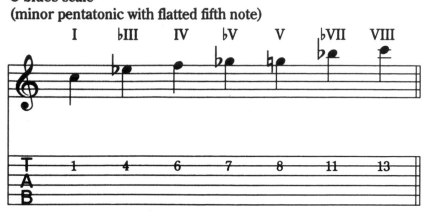

Solo 1a: *Please Excuse Me*

Our first backing track, "Please Excuse Me," originally comes from the *JamTrax* package entitled *More Blues JamTrax for Guitar*. This package is the sequel to our very first and most successful package, *Blues JamTrax for Guitar*. We start off in the key of E major, and you'll see from some of the following scales and techniques and from some of the licks throughout these solos that we can use notes from both major- and minor-mode scales. "Please Excuse Me" is a typical blues jam in the style of Eric Clapton's version of "Before You Accuse Me" from his *Journeyman* disk.

E Minor Pentatonic Box Pattern

Memorize this E minor pentatonic scale pattern, and practice playing it with both strict down and alternate picking.

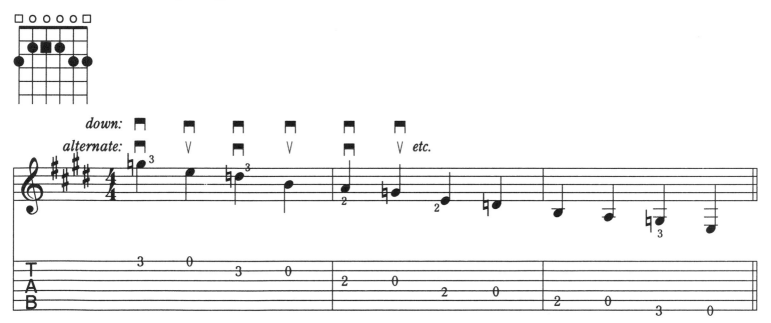

E Blues Scale

Adding the *flat five* (♭5) to the E box pattern produces the E *blues scale*.

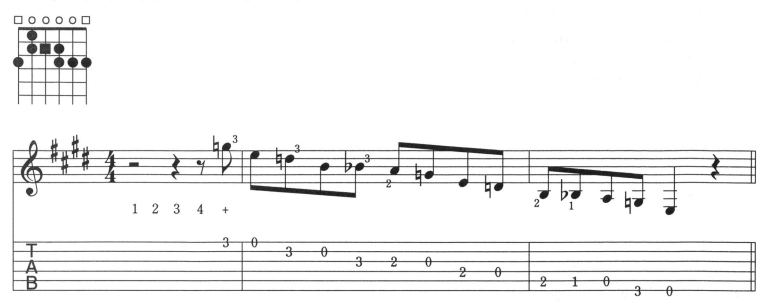

Slides

A *slide* line that connects two tied notes indicates that the first note should be picked before sliding the fret-hand finger to the second, unpicked note. Do not release pressure on the string while sliding.

Please Excuse Me **Solo 1a**

Moderate shuffle (♩♩ = ♩ ♪)

Intro (backing track guitar and drum cue)

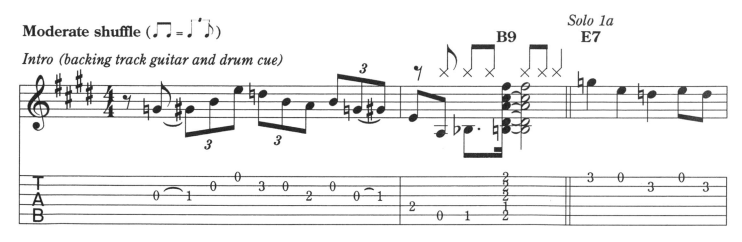

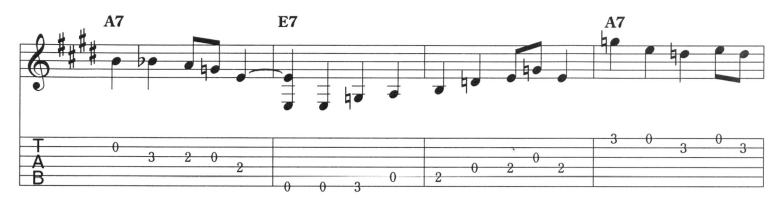

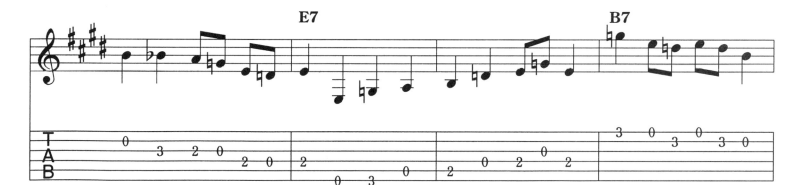

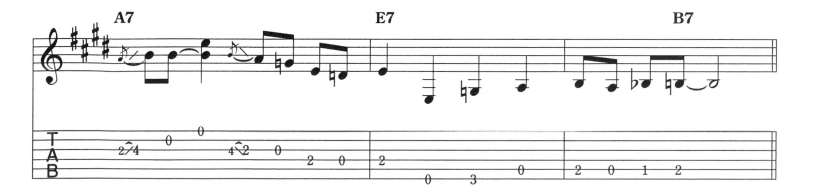

Solo 1b: Scales and Techniques

E Box Pattern with Mixed Major and Minor Third Notes

This variation on the minor pentatonic scale alters the box scale so that it can be used more effectively when playing in decidedly major keys. Our one admittedly oversimplified rule which addresses the important issue of when (and when not) to use the major or minor third is that the minor third note may be played over a major chord but, the major third note sounds awful when played over a minor chord. Again, this is quite an oversimplification of scale application, but our goal here is to present a few basic scales, concepts, and riff patterns that can be used to solo in many different musical situations.

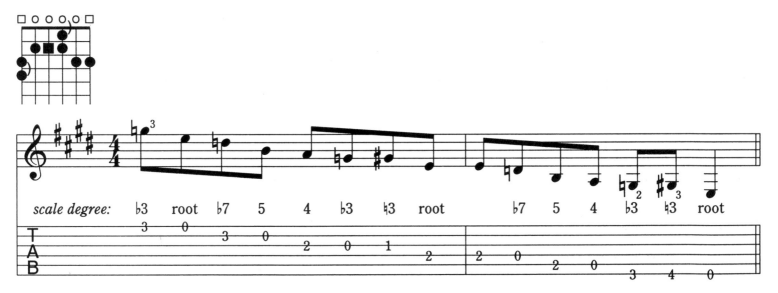

Hammerons and Pulloffs

The *hammerons* in measure 1 involve an open note and the second fret-hand finger. First play the open note, then sound the second note by "hammering" the higher note with a fret-hand fingertip. The *pulloffs* in measure 2 also involve an open note and the second fret-hand finger. This time the first note is fretted and picked but the second note is sounded by "plucking" the string or *pulling off* with the fret-hand fingertip.

Various Bend, Release, and Pulloff Combinations

Play these *bends* by playing the grace note and then immediately bending the string (toward the middle of the fretboard) until the second pitch is heard. The release directs you to keep downward pressure on the bent string while releasing the bend, until the original pitch is heard again. Measure 3 has mixed major- and minor-third bends.

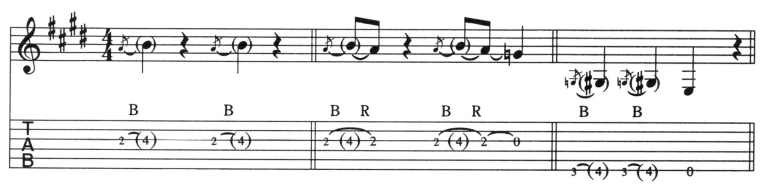

The Quarter-Tone Bend

For an explanation of the *quarter-tone bend* see the "Legend of Musical Symbols."

C9 and B9 Chords

These two chords are the same chord shape played in two different positions. Try moving this chord shape up the neck, placing the chord's root note on each of the fifth-string natural notes.

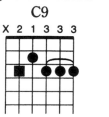 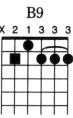

Please Excuse Me **Solo 1b**

Solo 1c: Patterns and Techniques

E Box Pattern with Flat Five Notes and Mixed Major-
   and Minor-Third Notes

Mixed Major/Minor Riff

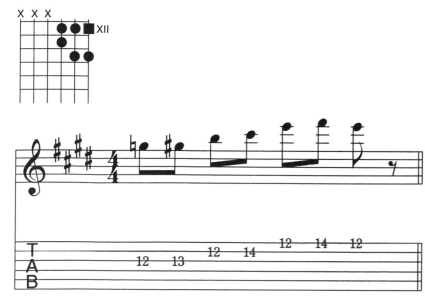

Mixed Major/Minor Thirds Riff in Four Locations

Bends and the Bend-Release-Pulloff Combination

These represent the various bends you'll encounter in Solo 1c. Here the final bend is combined with a release and a pulloff.

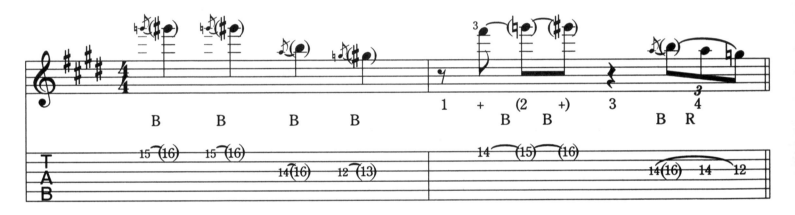

Various Slides

Listen to the audio track to hear the subtle differences in the sound of these slides.

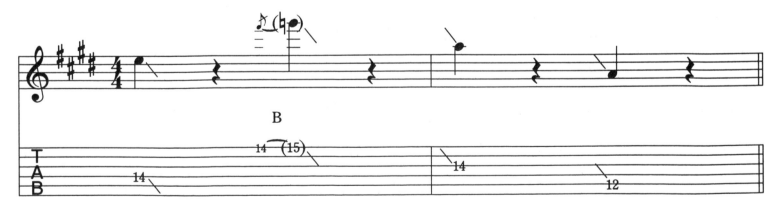

Various Hammerons

Measure 1 involves mixed major- and minor-mode notes. Measure 2 features several major/minor third combinations.

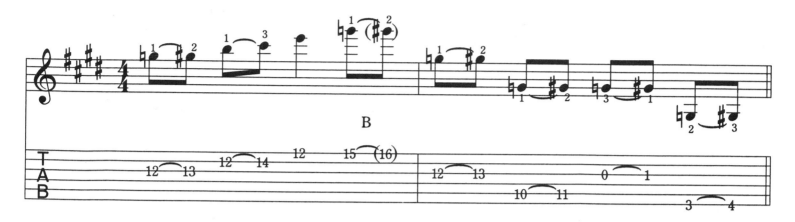

Pulloffs

Double Stops/Hammeron Riffs

A *double stop* is a two note chord. Here, we combine a few of them and include a hammeron in the second measure.

Please Excuse Me Solo 1c

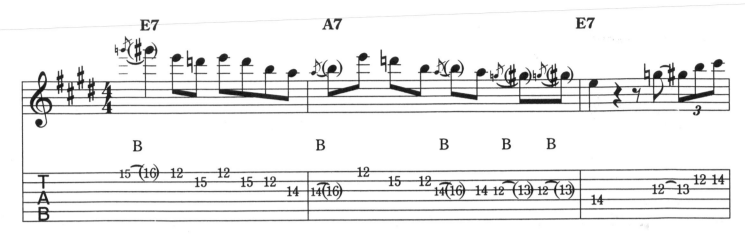

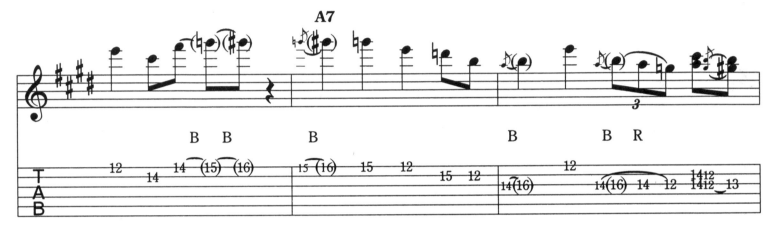

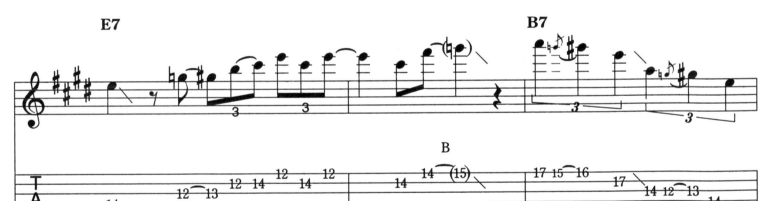

Chord Chart for *Please Excuse Me*

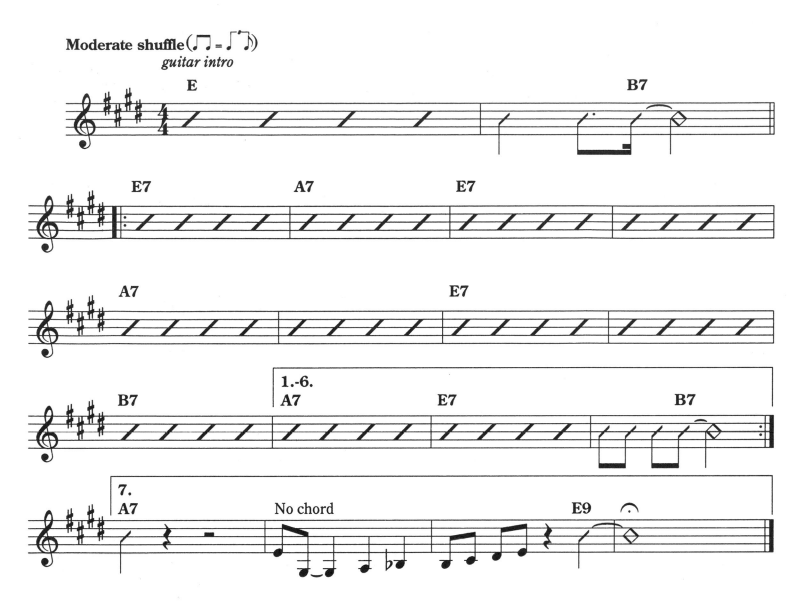

Legend of Musical Symbols

Hammeron: Play the first note normally, then sound the second (higher) note by bringing down a different fret-hand finger. Do not squeeze the second note. Think of hammering and then holding the wood underneath the hammered note.

Pulloff: Play the first note normally, then rapidly pull away the fret-hand finger that is holding down that note so that the second, lower note can sound. You should already be fingering the lower note with another fret-hand finger.

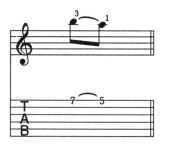

Bend: Finger the lower note indicated, then bend the string until you achieve the pitch of the higher note in parentheses. The note in parentheses is not actually fretted; it is written to tell you what the pitch of the bent note should be.

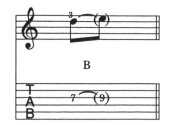

Release, or reverse bend: Finger the lower note indicated, but before striking the string, bend it so that the pitch of the higher note (in parentheses) will sound first when you pick the string. After picking, relax the bend until the original pitch sounds. A release often comes directly after a bend. Do not pick the note to be released if it is tied to the previous note.

Slide (to a definite pitch): Play the first note; then, without releasing pressure on the string, slide the fret-hand finger to the second note. If there is no tie, pick the second note.

Slide (to an indefinite pitch): When a slide line leads to no other note, slide up or down a few frets releasing finger pressure at the end of the slide.

Unison Bend: Finger the note, not in parentheses, with your first fret-hand finger while fingering the grace-note pitch with another fret-hand finger. Then pick both strings while at the same time bending the grace note until it's pitch matches that of the note on the higher string.

Vibrato: As you play the indicated note, smoothly and rhythmically move the string back and forth across the fretboard with the fret-hand finger, so that the pitch of the note wavers slightly up and down. Another kind of vibrato is achieved by simply shaking the fret-hand finger from side to side while playing the indicated note.

Trill: Play the first note, then hammer on to the second note and pull off to the first note in quick succession as many times as you can for the duration of the first note.

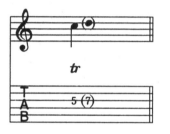

Quarter-tone bend: The *quarter tone* (or step) is, as it sounds, half of a half step. Smaller intervals than a half step can be sounded by bending. Finger the indicated note, then bend the string until the pitch rises a quarter tone, (just "nudge" the pitch of the note a little bit higher).